P9-CFS-739

Christmas COOKIES

Scrumptious Recipes with Decoration Tips

by Linda Curtis
Recipes created by Sassy Hall
Photographs by John Pemberton

Weidenfeld & Nicolson
New York

A TERN BOOK

Copyright © 1987 by Tern Enterprises, Inc.

All rights reserved. No part of this publication may be reproduced, stored in a retrieval system, or transmitted, in any form or by any means, electronic, mechanical, photocopying, recording, or otherwise, without the prior written permission of the copyright owner.

Published by Weidenfeld & Nicolson, New York
A Division of Wheatland Corporation
10 East 53rd Street
New York, New York 10022

ISBN 1-55584-134-1

Library of Congress Cataloging-in-Publication Data
available upon request.

CHRISTMAS COOKIES
Scrumptious Recipes with Decoration Tips
was prepared and produced by
Tern Enterprises, Inc.
15 West 26th Street
New York, New York 10010

Editor: Nancy Kalish
Art Director/Designer: Rod Gonzalez
Photo Editor: Philip Hawthorne
Production Manager: Karen L. Greenberg
Photographer: John Pemberton
Stylist: Richard Des Jardins

Typeset by BPE Graphics, Inc.
Color separations by Hong Kong Scanner Craft Company Ltd.
Printed and bound in Hong Kong by Leefung Asco Printers Ltd.

First Edition 1987

10 9 8 7 6 5 4 3 2 1

Dedicated to Allison and Christopher Hall

TABLE OF CONTENTS

SPECIAL COOKIES TO GIVE AS GIFTS
PAGE · 36

Double Delight Bourbon Balls
Christmas Wreaths
Cream Cheese Cookies
Pinwheels
Chocolate Cheesecake Chunks
Pecan Triangles
Twinkles
Poinsettias

COOKIES KIDS LOVE TO MAKE...
AND EAT
PAGE · 54

Sugar Santas
Candy Cane Cookies
Swiss Chalets
Chocolate Crispers
Chocolate Chip Meringues
Peanut Butter Balls
Snowmen
Children's Delight

INTRODUCTION

Nothing brings to mind holiday warmth and festivity more than the fragrance of delicious Christmas cookies baking in the oven. Serving them is a wonderful way to say welcome. This season, you can make these special cookies for family and friends—for home entertaining as well as for gift giving—even if you are a beginning baker. Some are even easy enough for kids to make! All you need is some basic baking tools, some time, and some decorating imagination. The rest is simple—just follow our how-tos to make the best-looking, best-tasting cookies ever.

The types of cookies featured are:
Bar: The cookie mixture is spread in a baking pan (like a cake). After baking, it is cut into squares, triangles, or other shapes.
Drop: The dough is dropped by spoonfuls onto baking sheets. These cookies are simple to make and can take on a variety of forms, depending on the decorations you choose.
Cutout: These cookies get their well-defined shapes from special tools. The

dough is rolled out flat, then cut into shapes using cookie cutters or cardboard patterns and a sharp knife.

Hand Molded: These cookies take the most time, but are also the most unique since they are shaped entirely by hand. The only limitation here is your imagination—they can be fancy and decorative or crafted into simple shapes.

The basic cookie dough ingredients are certainly simple enough to work with: butter, sugar, eggs, flour, leavening agents (like baking powder and soda), spices, and flavorings like vanilla. Once you get the knack of working with the dough to shape it into the forms you want, decorating cookies is easy and can be a fun project for the whole family.

HELPFUL HINTS

1. Be sure to give yourself enough preparation time. For some cookies, you will need to make the dough the day before and chill it overnight. Others will require extra time to cut and mold, while still others will need to be decorated after baking. Determine which kind of cookies you will make and how much time each will need—do not ruin the fun of making holiday cookies by feeling rushed.

2. Invest in some baker's tools such as rolling pin covers and pastry cloths. You will find they are well worth the extra cents by preventing raw dough from sticking as it is rolled out.

3. For those cookies needing already chilled dough, remember to divide dough into four even, individually wrapped sections before chilling so it is easier to work with and roll out.

4. Most cookie doughs should be mixed in the following sequence. First whip the butter and sugar together until creamy. Then beat in the eggs, flavorings, and any liquids. Next the flour, leavening agents, and any spices are stirred together, leaving nuts, chips, and any chunky ingredients to be mixed in last by hand.

5. Use all-purpose flour in these recipes, either bleached or unbleached. Do not use whole-wheat flour in these recipes.

6. While it is not necessary to sift your dry ingredients, it is important to measure them accurately. Use plastic or metal measuring cups specifically designed to measure dry, not liquid, ingredients. Gently spoon the dry ingredient into the cup; do not pack it down. Level off the cup with a flat knife or spatula. Brown sugar is the exception to this rule. It should be packed down firmly into the cup with your fingers, then leveled.

7. Whenever possible, use only butter in the recipes; butter is richer than margarine and your cookies will taste better.

8. Unless otherwise indicated, butter should be softened before using it to make the cookie dough in order to ensure a creamy consistency. Leave it out of the refrigerator until it reaches room temperature, or soften it on top of a warm oven.

9. When unspecified nuts are called for, you can use walnuts, almonds, hazelnuts, pecans—whichever type you prefer. To grind the nuts you will need a blender, food processor, or hand-held chopper.

10. Use only flat cookie sheets—ones with sides on them do not allow for even heating and browning. Flat sheets also make it easier to remove the cookies once baked. Make sure the sheets are cool before baking so the fat in the dough does not melt, resulting in flat cookies.

11. Leave at least 1 inch between each piece of dough when placing it on the cookie sheet. In addition, center the cookie sheets on the rack in the middle of the oven. This allows for even baking.

12. It is a good idea to turn the cookie sheets around at least once while baking. The ideal time is when cookies are about half done.

13. After baking, transfer the cookies with a spatula onto a dry rack to cool. You can also use a brown paper bag, laid flat; this will absorb any grease from the cookies. Arrange them in a single layer, not stacked one on top of another. Always let cookies cool completely before decorating.

14. If you plan to store plain cookies before decorating, put them into airtight tins or containers and leave them in a cool place; refrigeration is not necessary.

15. You can freeze raw cookie dough in most cases. Let it defrost fully in the refrigerator before rolling out, however, or it will crack. Most baked cookies can also be frozen successfully. To freeze baked cookies, place them in a single layer on an uncovered cookie sheet and freeze. Then remove and stack in freezer-proof containers. Thaw at room temperature for two hours before serving.

16. You can also make and store icing and frosting before decorating; just leave it in the mixing bowl. Cover with a damp cloth or dampened paper towel. Wrap this covered bowl with plastic wrap and store in the refrigerator. The dampened towels will help the frosting retain moisture so it will not dry out.

EQUIPMENT LIST

Large, medium-size, and small bowls
Wooden spoons
Liquid-ingredient measuring cups
Dry-ingredient measuring cups
Measuring spoons
Electric stationary or hand mixer
Rolling pin
Rolling pin covers
Pastry cloths (or large cutting board)
Waxed paper
Cookie cutters
Cookie molds
Spatula
Cookie sheets
Baking pans
Saucepans
Pastry bags (for decoration)
Cooling racks
Small spatula (for icing)

SPECIAL INGREDIENTS

Assorted colored sugars
Cinnamon "red hots"
Mixed candied fruits
Silver candy balls
Food coloring

TRADITIONAL CHRISTMAS COOKIES FROM AROUND THE WORLD

CLARITA'S BUTTERFLIES

MEXICO

These light-as-air confections are made with hot butterfly-shaped cookie irons dipped into sweet batter. The cookie irons and holders are available for a few dollars at cookware shops.

2 eggs
2 teaspoons granulated sugar
½ cup milk
½ cup beer
1 cup all-purpose flour
½ teaspoon salt
1 tablespoon lemon extract
Vegetable oil for deep frying
Confectioners sugar

Beat eggs lightly in a large bowl. Add sugar, milk, and beer. In a separate bowl, blend flour and salt and add to egg mixture; beat until smooth. Beat in lemon extract. Fill a 5-quart frying pan or large pot with oil until two-thirds full. Heat oil to 400° over medium-high heat. Dip cookie iron into hot oil; carefully remove and drain excess oil on paper towels. Then dip iron into the batter, covering iron almost to the top, and leave in for 3 seconds. Plunge the batter-covered iron into hot oil until lightly browned, about 1 minute. Ease butterfly off iron with fork and drain on paper towels. (Since the first few butterflies may stick to the iron, you may have to loosen them with a knife to remove. As you continue to make them they will come off more easily.) Sift confectioners sugar over cookies when all are made. Serve immediately.

YIELD: *About 3 dozen*

PEPPARKAKOR
(Gingerbread Boys)
SWEDEN

3½ cups all-purpose flour
1 teaspoon baking soda
¼ teaspoon salt
1½ teaspoons ground ginger
1½ teaspoons ground cinnamon
1 teaspoon ground cloves
½ cup butter, softened
¾ cup granulated sugar
1 egg
¾ cup molasses
1 teaspoon grated lemon peel

FROSTING:
⅓ cup egg whites
3¾ cups confectioners sugar

Blend flour with baking soda, salt, ginger, cinnamon, and cloves in a medium bowl. In a large bowl, beat butter and sugar at high speed until light and fluffy. Beat in egg, then molasses and lemon peel until well blended. With a wooden spoon, stir in flour mixture, then mix with a wooden spoon or knead with hands until smooth. Divide dough into four parts, wrap each in plastic, and refrigerate overnight.

Preheat oven to 375° and grease cookie sheets. Roll out one part of the dough at a time on a floured pastry cloth or board to ⅛-inch thickness. Cut into gingerbread boys with cookie cutters or with a floured knife and place on cookie sheets, spacing about 1 inch apart. With a sharp knife, make a small hole at the top of each cookie through which to thread a ribbon, if

desired. Bake 6 to 8 minutes or until lightly browned. Cool cookies on racks.

In the meantime, in a medium bowl at medium speed, beat egg whites and confectioners sugar to make a smooth, stiff frosting, about 1 minute. Cover with a damp cloth until ready to use.

To decorate cookies, spoon frosting into a pastry bag fitted with the smallest round tip. Work with bag about one-third full. Twisting bag with even pressure, pipe frosting along borders of cookies and within to form hair, features and clothing of gingerbread boys.

Let frosting dry, then store in a covered tin.

YIELD: *About 7 dozen, depending on size*

SPECULAAS

(Teddy Bear Cookies)
HOLLAND

3 cups all-purpose flour
1 1/2 teaspoons ground cinnamon
1 teaspoon ground cloves
1 teaspoon ground ginger
1/8 teaspoon baking powder
1/8 teaspoon salt
1 cup butter, softened
1 1/4 cups light brown sugar, packed
1 egg
1/2 cup sliced blanched almonds

Blend flour with spices, baking powder, and salt in a medium bowl. In a large bowl, beat butter and sugar at high speed until light and fluffy. Beat egg in well. With wooden spoon, stir in half the flour mixture, then add the remaining flour and almonds, mixing with a wooden spoon or kneading with hands. Divide dough into four parts, wrap in plastic, and refrigerate for several hours. (If you are using a mold, chill it as well.)

Preheat oven to 350° and grease two cookie sheets. Remove one quarter of the dough from refrigerator and flatten it with hands. Oil your mold and lightly flour it. Using fingers, press dough firmly into mold. Trim excess dough from mold with knife. Transfer cookie onto greased cookie sheet with spatula, spacing about 1 inch apart. Refrigerate dough trimmings to be rerolled later. Lightly flour—but do not oil—cookie mold. Repeat process with remaining dough. When cookie sheets are full, bake cookies for 20 to 25 minutes or until golden brown around the edges. Store in a covered tin.

YIELD: *About 2 dozen*

FRUITCAKE SQUARES

GERMANY

1 cup all-purpose flour
¼ teaspoon salt
½ teaspoon baking soda
½ teaspoon ground cinnamon
½ cup butter, softened
¾ cup granulated sugar
2 eggs
8 ounces pitted dates, chopped
¼ cup mixed candied fruit
½ cup red candied cherries, quartered
¾ cup chopped nuts
Red and green candied cherries, reserved for garnish

FROSTING:
1½ cups confectioners sugar
2½ tablespoons milk, more if necessary

Preheat oven to 375°. Grease and flour a 13 x 9 x 2-inch pan. In a small bowl, blend flour with salt, soda, and cinnamon. In a large bowl, beat butter, sugar, and eggs at medium speed until light and fluffy. Stir in flour, dates, candied fruits, quartered cherries, and nuts. Spread in prepared pan and bake 30 minutes until golden.

In the meantime, prepare the frosting by mixing together confectioners sugar and milk. Stir until smooth; then cover with a damp cloth until ready to use. Wait until cake has cooled, and cut into 2 x 1-inch bars. Then frost, using a butter knife or spatula and decorate with red and green candied cherries. Store, wrapped in waxed paper, in a covered tin.

YIELD: *About 4 dozen*

KRINGLES

DENMARK

Firm, pretzel-shaped cookies, these hand-molded Danish treats take a little more time to make. But their delicious, buttery, not-too-sweet taste makes them well worth the effort.

¾ cup butter
½ cup granulated sugar
3 hard-boiled egg yolks, sieved
1 raw egg
½ to ¾ teaspoon ground cardamom
2 cups all-purpose flour
1 egg white beaten with 1 tablespoon water
¼ cup coarse sugar (or coarsely crushed sugar cubes)

Preheat oven to 375° and grease several cookie sheets. In medium bowl with a wooden spoon or electric mixer, beat butter, sugar, egg yolks, raw egg and cardamom until light and fluffy. Stir in flour, mixing with hands until dough is stiff. Divide into four parts. Refrigerate, wrapped in plastic, for several hours. On floured surface, working with one part at a time, take a tablespoon of dough and roll into a 7-inch long thin rope. Shape into a pretzel and place on a greased cookie sheet. Continue to make pretzels until dough is used up, spacing 2 inches apart on cookie sheets. Brush with beaten egg white, then sprinkle with coarse sugar. Bake 10 to 12 minutes until golden. Cool on racks and store in a covered tin.

YIELD: *About 2 1/2 dozen*

TESSIE'S ALMOND CRESCENTS

AMERICA

These buttery, nutty delights are easy to make and are best eaten soon after baking. The combination of almonds and chocolate glaze make them a delicious, elegant cookie dessert.

1¾ cups (3½ sticks) butter
½ cup granulated sugar
1 teaspoon vanilla
4 cups all-purpose flour
1 cup chopped blanched almonds

GLAZE:
½ cup semisweet chocolate bits
1 tablespoon butter

Preheat oven to 350°. In a large bowl, beat butter, sugar, and vanilla until light and fluffy. Mix in flour and nuts and knead until smooth, about 5 minutes. Refrigerate for several hours. Using a teaspoon of dough at a time, roll in the palm of your hand to the size of a finger (about 2½ inches long); shape into a crescent. Space crescents about 1 inch apart on ungreased cookie sheets and bake for 8 minutes. Cool on racks.

To make the glaze, gently melt chocolate and butter together in a double boiler over low heat. Let cool slightly. Dip one end of each crescent into the chocolate mixture until well coated. Store, between layers of waxed paper, in a covered tin.

YIELD: *About 5 dozen*

CHROSCHICKI
(Bow Ties)
POLAND

These bow tie-shaped cookies from Poland are fun to eat, even though they may require a bit of patience to make. The secret to their light, delicate flavor is the unique, yet delicious, combination of sour cream and a bit of whiskey.

6 egg yolks
3 tablespoons granulated sugar
2¾ cups all-purpose flour
½ cup sour cream
1 tablespoon vanilla
1 tablespoon rye whiskey
Vegetable shortening for deep frying
Confectioners sugar

Beat egg yolks and granulated sugar until light and fluffy. Add flour and sour cream alternately until well combined. Add vanilla and whiskey. Knead about 5 minutes until dough does not stick to fingers; divide dough in half, wrap in plastic, and chill for 2 hours.

Roll dough out to ⅛-inch thickness. Cut into 4 x 1½-inch strips. Cut a lengthwise slit in the middle of each strip. Bring one end through this slit to form a bow tie. Fry in a large pot or deep fryer filled with vegetable shortening, heated to 400°, for about 1 minute on each side until lightly browned. Drain on paper towels, then sprinkle with confectioners sugar.

YIELD: *About 6 dozen*

RUGELACH

ISRAEL

1 cup butter
2 cups all-purpose flour
1 egg yolk
¾ cup sour cream
¾ cup granulated sugar
1 teaspoon ground cinnamon
¾ cup chopped walnuts
¼ cup butter, melted

Cut butter into flour using two knives, as if making a pie crust. In a separate bowl, beat egg yolk and sour cream well, then add to flour mixture. Mix until blended. Divide dough into three parts. Cover with plastic and refrigerate at least 3 hours.

Prepare filling by combining sugar, cinnamon, and walnuts. Preheat oven to 375°.

Working with one portion at a time, roll dough into circle ⅛-inch thick. Brush each circle lightly with melted butter and spread one-third of the filling on each. Cut each circle into 16 wedges, like a pizza. Starting from the large end of each wedge, roll up toward point, jelly-roll fashion. Place cookies on un-greased cookie sheets and bake 15 minutes or until lightly browned. Cool on racks and store in covered tins.

YIELD: *About 4 dozen*

SPECIAL
COOKIES TO
GIVE AS GIFTS

DOUBLE DELIGHT
BOURBON BALLS

These cookies are a chocolate lover's delight, with a taste of bourbon whiskey for a sophisticated touch. They are the perfect gift to bring along to a holiday party.

1 package (6 ounces) semisweet chocolate bits
3 tablespoons corn syrup
½ cup bourbon
1 package (8 ounces) chocolate wafers, crushed
1 cup chopped nuts
½ cup confectioners sugar
⅓ cup chopped candied red cherries
Granulated sugar

Gently melt chocolate in a double boiler over low heat. Remove from heat and stir in syrup and bourbon; cool to room temperature. Meanwhile, in a large bowl, mix wafers, nuts, confectioners sugar, and cherries. Add the chocolate mixture and stir to blend. Let stand for 30 minutes. Shape into 1-inch balls with fingers. Roll in granulated sugar, then refrigerate, covered, until ready to pack for gift giving.

To present these as a pretty gift, place each ball in a small paper candy cup and arrange in a basket lined with colored tissue paper.

YIELD: *About 2½ dozen*

CHRISTMAS WREATHS

These do require a pastry bag to shape, but they make wonderful cookies to eat or hang on the Christmas tree with a pretty ribbon tied around them. Bake them even bigger and they are perfect to hang in windows and on doors.

1 package (8 ounces) cream cheese, softened
1 cup butter, softened
1 cup granulated sugar
1 teaspoon vanilla
2 cups all-purpose flour
Sliced red and green candied cherries

Preheat oven to 350°. In a medium bowl, beat cream cheese, butter, sugar, and vanilla together until light and fluffy. Stir in flour slowly until blended. Working with one cup of the mixture at at time, press through a pastry bag fitted with a scroll tip onto ungreased cookie sheets to form 1½-inch wreaths. (Use a larger scroll tip when making bigger wreaths.) Press cherries into dough for decoration, as shown in photo. Bake 12 minutes (15 minutes for larger cookies) or until lightly browned.

Store, or give as gifts, packed in a decorative tin between layers of waxed paper. Cover with colored tissue paper.

YIELD: *About 3 dozen 1½-inch wreaths*

CREAM CHEESE COOKIES

These creamy cookies melt in your mouth. Depending on the cookie cutters used, they can be made into varied shapes and sizes and decorated as desired.

1 package (8 ounces) cream cheese, softened
½ cup butter, softened
1 cup granulated sugar
1½ cups all-purpose flour
Colored sugar or sprinkles

Beat all ingredients together with a wooden spoon or electric mixer. Divide into fourths, wrap in plastic, and refrigerate overnight.

Preheat the oven to 350°. On a floured pastry cloth or other floured surface, roll out dough, one fourth at a time, to ⅛-inch thickness. Keep remaining dough refrigerated until ready to be rolled out. Cut into assorted shapes such as trees, bells, stars, and reindeer using cookie cutters. Place on ungreased cookie sheets about 1 inch apart. Sprinkle with colored sugar or sprinkles; bake 6 to 8 minutes until slightly golden around the edges. Cool on racks.

When packing these cookies to give as gifts, keep in mind that they are quite delicate. They are best arranged in a single layer in a flat basket that has been lined with colored cellophane or a doily. Cover with plastic wrap until delivery.

YIELD: *About 4 dozen*

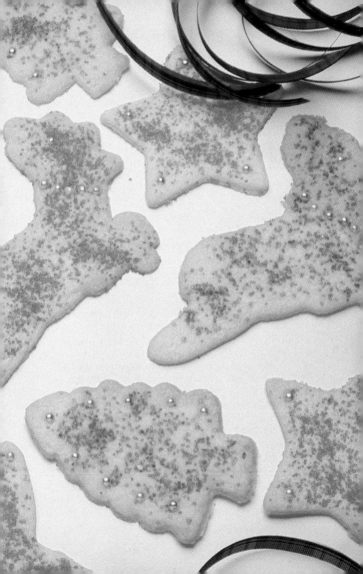

PINWHEELS

The streak of chocolate spiraling out from the center of these cookies makes them extra special. The dough can be prepared ahead of time and refrigerated; then simply slice and bake.

½ cup butter, softened
1 cup granulated sugar
1 egg
1 teaspoon vanilla
1¼ cups all-purpose flour
¼ teaspoon salt
1½ teaspoons baking powder
1 ounce unsweetened chocolate, melted

Preheat oven to 400° and grease several cookie sheets. In a large bowl, beat butter at medium speed until light and fluffy. Gradually add sugar, egg, and vanilla while continuing to beat. Sift flour into small bowl with salt and baking powder and add to butter mixture. Mix well. Divide dough in half and mix chocolate into one half. Wrap both halves in plastic and refrigerate for several hours.

Roll out plain and chocolate dough separately into oblongs about ⅛-inch thick. Place dark dough on top of light dough and roll up layers together, jelly-roll fashion. Wrap and refrigerate again overnight.

Cut roll into ⅛-inch thick slices and place on greased cookie sheet, spacing about 1 inch apart. Bake 8 minutes. Cool on racks.

Give these cookies layered in a shallow basket lined with colored tissue paper and tied up with a ribbon.

YIELD: *About 3 dozen*

CHOCOLATE CHEESECAKE CHUNKS

These creamy mini-cheesecakes sit atop a mouthwatering chocolate nut crust. Yet they are surprisingly simple to make. Just bake, then cut into bite-sized chunks for a taste of heaven.

½ cup butter
1¼ cups chocolate wafer crumbs (about 30 wafers)
1 cup chopped nuts
2 packages (3 ounces each) cream cheese, softened
⅓ cup granulated sugar
⅓ cup unsweetened cocoa powder
1 egg
1 teaspoon vanilla

Preheat oven to 350°. Melt butter in 9-inch square baking pan. Stir in crumbs and ½ cup nuts. Press to cover bottom of pan. In small bowl, beat cream cheese, sugar, cocoa, egg, and vanilla at medium speed until smooth. Pour over crust and sprinkle with remaining ½ cup nuts. Bake 20 minutes. Let stand at room temperature 2 hours. Cut into 1-inch squares with a sharp knife. Store, covered, in refrigerator.

These cookies are best presented in a single layer on a large round flat tray or basket lined with colored cellophane or a doily. Cover with plastic wrap to keep cookies in place until delivery.

YIELD: *81 chunks*

PECAN TRIANGLES

Like the best pecan pies, these cookies are sweet and rich, with a pleasing nutty flavor. Cut them into triangles and pop them into your mouth.

1⅓ cups all-purpose flour
½ cup plus 2 tablespoons brown sugar, packed
½ cup butter, softened
2 eggs
½ cup light corn syrup
1 cup chopped pecans
2 tablespoons butter, melted
1 teaspoon vanilla
⅛ teaspoon salt
Confectioners sugar

Preheat oven to 350° and grease a 9-inch square baking pan. In a small bowl, mix flour and the 2 tablespoons brown sugar. Work in ½ cup butter with fingers until dough begins to hold together. Press onto bottom of greased pan. Bake 12 to 15 minutes. Cool.

In medium bowl, beat the ½ cup brown sugar and eggs until light and fluffy. Beat in corn syrup, pecans, melted butter, vanilla, and salt. Pour on crust. Bake 25 minutes or until edges are lightly browned. Cool for 2 hours.

Sprinkle cake with confectioners sugar. Cut into 3-inch squares. Cut each square in half to make a triangle. Store layered between sheets of waxed paper in a tightly covered tin. For gift giving, use a decorated tin.

YIELD: *18*

TWINKLES

These are like star-shaped linzer tarts. You will need large and small star cookie cutters to make these double-decker delights.

2½ cups all-purpose flour
1 teaspoon baking powder
¼ teaspoon salt
¾ cup butter, softened
1 cup granulated sugar
2 eggs
1 teaspoon vanilla
6 tablespoons strawberry preserves

Blend flour, baking powder, and salt in a small bowl. In a large bowl, beat butter and sugar at medium speed until light and fluffy. Beat in eggs and vanilla well. Divide dough into three parts, wrap in plastic, and refrigerate 3 hours.

Preheat oven to 350° and grease several cookie sheets. On floured surface, roll one third dough at a time to ⅛-inch thickness. Cut dough with 2¾-inch star-shaped cookie cutter. With 1¼-inch star-shaped cookie cutter, cut out the centers of half the larger stars. Place on a greased cookie sheet, spacing about 1 inch apart, and bake 6 to 8 minutes. Cool on racks.

Spread 1 teaspoon of preserves in the center of the star cookies without cutouts. Place a cookie with a cutout on top, lining up the star's points on both cookies as shown in photo. Store in covered tin.

For gift giving, place cookies in flat basket or on tray lined with tissue paper in a single layer, slightly over-lapping at edges. Cover basket or tray with plastic wrap to keep cookies in place.

YIELD: *About 18*

POINSETTIAS

2½ cups all-purpose flour
¾ teaspoon salt
1 cup butter, softened
1 cup confectioners sugar
1 egg
1 teaspoon almond extract
1 teaspoon vanilla
Red decorating sugar
Silver candy balls

Blend flour and salt in small bowl. In medium bowl, beat butter and sugar until light and fluffy. Beat in egg, almond extract, and vanilla well. Stir in flour to mix well. Divide dough into fourths, wrap in plastic, and refrigerate overnight.

Preheat oven to 350° and grease several cookie sheets. On a floured surface, roll out dough one fourth at a time to ⅛-inch thickness. Cut into 2-inch squares. Working with one square at a time, make a ¾-inch cut from each corner running diagonally toward the center. Fold in alternate corners toward center of cookie (as in photo), creating a pinwheel effect. Place on greased cookie sheets, spacing about 1 inch apart. Repeat with remaining dough.

Sprinkle center of each cookie with red sugar and place a silver candy ball in the middle. Bake 8 to 10 minutes. Cool on racks.

Since these cookies are extremely delicate, pack them carefully in a single layer in a flat basket or on a tray lined with tissue paper. Tie it with a ribbon and you have a lovely and festive gift.

YIELD: *About 3½ dozen*

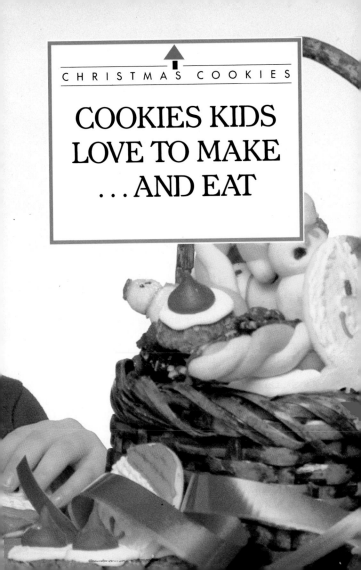

COOKIES KIDS
LOVE TO MAKE
...AND EAT

CANDY CANE COOKIES

These colorful, fun-to-make cookies taste of mint and are pretty enough to hang on the tree.

2½ cups all-purpose flour
½ teaspoon salt
1 cup butter, softened
1 cup confectioners sugar
1 egg
1 teaspoon peppermint extract
1 teaspoon vanilla
Red food coloring

Preheat oven to 350°. Blend flour and salt in a small bowl. In a large bowl, beat butter and sugar until light and fluffy. Beat in egg and extracts well, then stir in flour and salt. Divide dough in half and color one half with 8 drops red food coloring; refrigerate, wrapped in plastic, for 2 hours. Working with 1 teaspoon of dough at a time, form 5-inch-long, pencil-thin cylinders of each color. Twist one cylinder of each color together to look like a candy cane. Bake 12 to 15 minutes. Cool on racks and store in covered tins.

YIELD: *About 4 dozen*

SWISS CHALETS

2½ cups all-purpose flour
½ teaspoon baking soda
1 teaspoon baking powder
½ teaspoon salt
1½ teaspoons ground cinnamon
1 teaspoon ground ginger
½ teaspoon ground cloves
¼ teaspoon freshly grated nutmeg
½ cup butter, softened
½ cup granulated sugar
1 egg
½ cup molasses

DECORATIONS:
Frosting (see page 56)
Silver candy balls

Blend flour, baking soda and powder, salt, and spices in medium bowl. In large bowl, beat butter and sugar at medium speed until light and fluffy. Beat in egg well, then beat in molasses. Stir in flour mixture to blend well. Divide dough into three parts, wrap in plastic, and refrigerate 3 hours.

Preheat oven to 350°. On a floured surface, roll out dough, one third at a time, to ⅛-inch thickness. With 2 x 1-inch house-shaped cookie cutter, cut out cookies and place on ungreased cookie sheet, about 1 inch apart. Bake 5 to 6 minutes. Cool on racks.

Make frosting as described in the recipe on page 56, then spread on cookies (or pipe on, using a pastry bag). Decorate as desired. Store in a covered tin.

YIELD: 3 dozen

CHOCOLATE CRISPERS

Kids will enjoy making these chocolate, chewy treats from start to finish! They are free-form drop cookies that get extra flavor zip from the sweet decorations you use on them.

1 package (6 ounces) semisweet chocolate bits
½ cup light corn syrup
1 can (3 ounces) chow mein noodles
Cinnamon "red hots"
Silver candy balls
Candied red and green cherries, chopped or slivered

Combine chocolate bits, corn syrup, and 1 tablespoon water in a double boiler and heat over low heat until chocolate melts. Remove from heat and stir to blend. Add noodles and mix. Drop by teaspoonfuls onto cookie sheets covered with waxed paper. Decorate tops with candies and cherries. Refrigerate to harden for 1½ hours. Store in covered tins at room temperature and eat within three days of making.

YIELD: *About 3 dozen*

PEANUT BUTTER BALLS

These chewy chill-and-serve treats combine the rich taste of peanut butter with the delicate sweetness of honey and coconut. And because it is very easy to prepare and involves no work at the stove, this recipe is a great way to introduce even a small child to cookie making.

1 cup peanut butter
½ cup honey
1 cup quick oats
1 cup chopped, mixed dried fruit
1 cup shredded sweetened coconut

In a large bowl, combine all ingredients except for coconut. Mix well with wooden spoon and shape into 1-inch balls. Roll balls in coconut. Serve immediately or chill. Store, wrapped in waxed paper, in a covered tin.

YIELD: *About 4 dozen*

SNOWMEN

These snowmen are even more fun to build than the usual kind—and are certainly tastier. Frost on the hats and mufflers, and do not forget the raisin eyes and belly buttons.

1 cup butter, softened
½ cup granulated sugar
1 teaspoon vanilla
2 cups all-purpose flour
Raisins, coarsely chopped
Frosting (see page 56) with 8 drops green
food coloring added
Chocolate chips
3 tablespoons confectioners sugar

Preheat oven to 325°. In a large bowl, beat butter, sugar, and vanilla until light and fluffy. Stir in flour to blend well. For each snowman, shape dough into 3 balls, measuring 1 inch, ¾ inch, and ½ inch. Place on ungreased cookie sheet with the sides of the balls touching and press together gently; space snowmen about 1 inch apart. Insert raisins for eyes (and belly button, if desired). Bake 18 minutes. Cool on racks.

Prepare frosting as directed in the recipe on page 56 and fill pastry bag, fitted with writing tip, one-third full. Decorate cookies with frosting and chips as shown in picture or as desired. Sprinkle lightly with confectioners sugar. Store in covered tins.

YIELD: *About 2 dozen*

CHILDREN'S DELIGHT

These peanut butter oatmeal drops are topped off with miniature mountains of chocolate kisses, incorporating just about everything a kid could want into one cookie. They require a few minutes at the stove, but no baking.

2 cups granulated sugar
¼ cup unsweetened cocoa powder
½ cup milk
½ cup butter
½ cup peanut butter
½ teaspoon vanilla
2½ cups quick oats
Chocolate chips or chocolate kisses
Frosting (see page 56)

In a saucepan, bring sugar, cocoa, milk, and butter to a boil, stirring. Cook 1 minute, then remove from heat. Add peanut butter and vanilla and mix well. Pour over the oats in a large bowl. Mix again, and drop by teaspoonfuls onto a cookie sheet lined with waxed paper. Prepare frosting as directed in the recipe on page 56. Flatten slightly with fingers and decorate with frosting and a chocolate chip or chocolate kiss. Chill for 1 hour. Serve immediately or store, covered, in refrigerator.